The Boy From The Green Cabaret
Tells Of His Mother

Some of these poems have previously appeared in: *Asylum,*
Cutely, Stand, Nicely, Mainly, Grosseteste Review, Target,
Flame, The English Intelligencer, Origins/Diversions,
The Assassinators Broadsheet, Collection 2,
Fred's Broadsheet, Resuscitator, Open, Vogue, and Makaris
and have been read on: Tyne Tees Television and
B.B.C. Third Programme.
The sequence, *The Boy From The Green Cabaret*
*Tells Of His Mother,** was published in an edition of one
hundred from Hastings, Sussex, October 1967

*The Boy is Rimbaud, and the *Cabaret Vert* is a pub in
Central France where he wrote a letter to his mother, and a poem

Barry MacSweeney

Poems 1965 to 1968

**The Boy From The Green Cabaret
Tells of His Mother**

DAVID McKAY COMPANY, INC.

NEW YORK

Library of Congress Catalog Card Number: 69-20208
MANUFACTURED IN THE UNITED STATES OF AMERICA

Contents

The autobiography of Barry MacSweeney

'Born in "The Village", Benwell, Newcastle On Tyne,
July 1948. Educated Rutherford Grammar School, best
subjects art & english. About 1963 picked up in France a
copy of Rimbaud's *Illuminations* and *The Drunken Boat*.
Then Baudelaire, Laforgue. Wrote first poems at school.
That was a cissy thing to do of course. Began job as
reporter on local evening paper. Met Basil Bunting, poet.
Met Tom Pickard and Jon Silkin. Showed Bunting *Walk*
poem, it came back sliced down to about 4 lines and a note:
Start again from there. My first real lesson. Reporting gave
me sense of what words could be: economy and just get
down the *needed* things, with no frills. Open to the city
and the country. You can walk out of Newcastle for half
and hour and be in greenery. The city gave words a
harshness, like the steel or coal. Then I wd flit off to little
stone cottage on the fells and fish for trout, and pick
mushrooms. & swim in the freshwater lakes. Began to
translate Laforgue, Cros, Corbiere.
1966–67: newspaper packed me off to Harlow Technical
College, Essex, on a full-time journalist diploma course.
An opposite life altogether. Synthetic new town, a dormi-
tory to London. Its population, commuters with a
vengeance. And the land was flat, that was a shock. An
utter antithesis to Newcastle. Everything was so clean
and clear-cut, and the people, they didn't *belong*, and
had no roots in the town. Oasis. It was impossible to get
involved. My eye, my colour/sluice became arbitrary
for the first time. It was merely a funnel, and events and
actions got a natural response from me. In Newcastle I
was always too involved, always leaving pieces of myself
against the walls. I wrote *The Boy From The Green
Cabaret* poems in Harlow, and some political things for
the first time. It was here I really woke up. Poems were
fast and often, but it was bitter and solitary too. Spent
days looking for some natural spot in the whole synthesis:
found it, a small duck pond with sluice and lily-pads and

foot-bridge. Told later it was one of the town planner's landscaping tricks.

Left here July 1967, *sans honneur*, carrying a bad character report in my hand & some poems, returned home to get the sack. But they didn't like the cut of my face either. Since then jobs as chief reporter in Cumberland, dole, reporter, social security, dole, gardener, dole. Now helps run Morden Tower poetry readings, and publishing posters and books. & of course writing poems. Wants to see poets get away from revisionism. Nobody returns in glory to Lucknow. and this is June, 1968, Newcastle.'

Poems

January 1965 to October 1966

To Lynn at Work whose Surname I don't know

The sun always goes down
like this between the
staithes of the High Level Bridge,
dragging a golden plate across
the sewage,
          and then breaking it
among the rooftops of the
wharf-side houses and stores,
bending yellow slivers
up the mast of the red tug,
and on the starlings in the
chimney nests,
nooked in the lampblack and grey
shipping offices
          above Sandgate.

the dusty navvies
back across the Tyne,
sledgehammer at red-brick walls in the heat,
and slate eves, lugging
concrete heaps and half-bricks
with knotted hankies on their broad heads.

pedestrians this way down to
Mosley Street and back to work.

now i think i will come to you
and ask you and pour the Tyne
and the sun's bangles in your
lips and hair and bathe your
hands
in
this evening.

looking for these dark bottles
over the pelmet under the wardrobe
these green bottles in roomcorners
in the loft   these peculiar places

down from the cathedral
this 10 o clock sun
warms the market cobbles
teeth hair legs hands
your eyes fingers tumble
onto the road   i rush out
pick them up

dusting these dark bottles
in the bath beneath the clock
house full of dark bottles
green bottles filling the
dark rooms   bottles full of you.

The Two Questions
The Two Places

I

a star reflection
from the oilstove grill
upon the cream
                ceiling
dark now in the late evening.
peggy lee sings
that her heart belongs to daddy.
one minute we kiss
the next i tell you
how indestructible and indomitable you are
(this terrible silence)
i feel wretched.
then i leap off the bed & point out
all the shadowy objects
all the green & grey shapes
in the room
                in french
you laugh
(we lie on the red cover
your breasts are the runs of my youth)

i in you
(a sort of pact)

2

the bright daffodils
in the orange teapot
with its long spout, the roughly hewn table
the scattered manuscripts and letters
a leather bound volume of byron
an article on basil torn from the scotsman,
half-loaves of brown bread, fore-arm long.
     poems by lorca,
then the bluegrey of the window
this
 & a peace
the first for three months or more.

On the Gap Left after Leaving

1

When the coast
was not the coast
and sea was a shell
and shell-life was man,
    before the entire march began,
there had you, all you have now.
    before a crow
    flew across
    corn-mill flats
past the flat, hard elements.
before Sammy the poacher
ever tramped Killop
with half a dozen rabbits in the bag,
while all these houses
were fields and cowlands,
before the Paniards
were tractor-tooth bitten,
scarred with 1966.

2

In linctus eyes
that tell stories
of other stolen hours
the early harrow struck sun
reflects scenes
of dull ochre, squinting
through the gables of Tudor stone
in the orchard's heart.

3

Sun lemons
blaze in bubbles
(old means,
new, intricate designs), on leaves
    where in winter
i traced your hair,
when windows were sculpted marble white,
with frost, nightly—
   —frozen.

Tree

the metal cloud banks
of October
at noon.
spoon sun,
paths of
golden and brown
dead leaves and
the sharp,
       fox-eye
razor branches
of a beech.

so cold
air breathing
with frost.

so cold,
beautiful
      tree.

Walk

Tynemouth priory stands
sepia walled
hunched in bony remnants
of a holy rood,
gaunt anatomy of stones

cliffs plait
light brown and black
into shapes
        above the splash
        of paddlers

wind hoys sea

on shore,

        glassing to a sand edge.

Tynemouth curls like a cat
along the coast

the liner carries
the breaking of sky

sea is not for yielding
except willeks

& pale
crabs,
    sold on rough tables
    (hewn as roughly as the fishers)
these fishing towns, crofts,
the lighthouse, foyboats, foymen—

They are allowed.

How soon before
coalfish
haddock
cod
are cold as diamond
in quayside barrels,
before the hull strikes
waves again?
        again.
How long before
trawler crews rest their lids,
how long till nostrils are salt clean,
& fingers no longer grapple with nylon?

Then,
will they perch
like condors,
stooping for catches
with catgut claws?

It is not
of fish,
        the sea
            consists,

            it is not
        of water.

Song: Bronchitis (for Paul)

Without a word,
a single sound
my brother crawls from behind me,

onto my sheets,
                    over my legs,
spans me with his young body
slides through the wall next to
my head
and coughs duets with the man
next-door until the sun comes up
when they sling mucus balls
at sparrows and robins

If It Were Winter

If it were winter
and snowy, I would
build a snowman,
with comb mouth,
eyes of dark blue buttons,
nose of carrot, pipe
of a toothbrush, as real
as 'The Thinker'.
But if you came
along,
        Ann,
asking if you could
knock it down,
after all my effort,
I would say yes.
Yes my love.

And after you had gone
I would secretly rebuild it,
and hide it from you.
(not wishing to hurt you)

When Van Gogh

When Van Gogh
the brilliant mad
painter tramped through Paris
(sunflowers, O sunflowers!)
after quarrelling
with Gauguin,

and heard starlings
above Sacre Coeur,

it went in one ear and
stayed there.

Dr Zhivago, Love Poem

I leapt into the aisle
hand out

ready to wipe her tears
before they fell

They arrested me for
tearing another
Cinemascope screen with intent

The Vivienne Poems

For Andrei Voznesensky, for her

I am irregular as poker chips.

Her body is mine,
12-string guitar,
Medieval flute.

                (a Matryoshki doll, I find you,
                    peel you like a tangerine)
She glows in ballet
   of the life she leads,

   firebirding me.

Ice on the river
river flows deep,

never seen the icicle eyes
of those three dead

Three bullets,
                three neat death holes
                ladybirds on the brow)

                two duels, a suicide.

Burning cannon of loins
blasts me like eggshell.
Clay fires birds eyes.
Water, stone,
                tungsten wings beat a shadow
over the lives of three dead Russians.

You make up for their loss—
   Russia doesn't know.

You make me forget turbulence,

the North Sea in me,

      touch me with your fingers
      look to me for love

Bored with bad poetry
I'm off to Russia,
drink vodka with poets there.

Ball-points and bayonets
are singular in Moscow!
      —gallop through the Caucasus
            with Lermontov's ghost.
My love mis-understands,

         but her name is sweeter
      than bells of funerals,
        her tongue quicker than
    a beam,
         pelvis moist as moss. lips to blood
I am yours,
more than a swallow to
  the sky, my love,
more than a swallow to
  the clouds.

Tell me you will lie with no other.
In case I should topple,
Like a clown
        do
          crazy
acrobatics,

Steady my heart with yours

  put away old scenes.

The Sweet Ability

the omnipresence
of each other and
objects.

we have a bed
four walls

two or three
pink sheets

a sparrow
in the eves

but above all
we have

the ability
to undress
one another, lie

naked under
musical sheets

Such a Lot

so much depends
upon

my left hand on
your right
nipple,

my right hand on
your backside,

so much
on three words we
know what
they are

so much on your
fingers in my storm of
cock hair

a lot
dear lady
depends

on us

Fountains

fountains
  spray
    with
      watery teeth

collects light
  in vertical
  gold rooms

  listening
  intently to the
    song of cold
liquid

'The sheaf opening
    Into a thousand flowers'

(thighs a ghost harp
  fingers a wraith
  of lace
  streaming
like gin
  across your skin)

drizzle
  kisses
    your skin

you stretch
  over me

  a twig
slippery

shining like
a vast
    raindrop

For A Pale Time, No Matter

1

Time of breaking glass   anonymous rivers counties
lost maps.   scrolls crumble, red letters
fade to indistinct pink, families wandering nameless
      fireless, foodless
      uniform colours
      birds will fly only

2

Sun strokes buildings in Clement Attlee Square
concrete broad walks   flatly constructed areas
openspace plans to hand suggesting no walls or fences
      no birds *live* here
      crumbs are perfunctory
      housing rows in gentle arcs
      steaming kitchen grills
      setting scenes
for a pale day

3

Love is colourful.
Red, blonde, white, mustard, smells of leather and polish,
holds implements, rows a weal in the smoothness of
      days (like pebbles)
      harrows the quietness of monotony
      springs into eyes/
            young heads swaying
            with promise

            until circumstance acts.

Love *may* be compared with a rainbow, but that is romance
and not what Love is. Is attraction, argument, spring coming
from death of winter, end of one year, beginning of an age,
                              attitude of war,
                              clasped memory,
                              howed earth
and mine,
what it is, is enough.

Song

I make marigold chains for yr breasts,
sleep on pigskin,
thigh to thigh

    our kids
are tall, silver haired
        spear rabbit
    with willow-
                wand

I Shant Come Back if You Keep Blowing, Blues

The oil-heater hums, hot
against our sweating heads
we have lain naked on these
thin sheets an hour or more
The church bell strikes three

Time goes on but we stay here
flowers curl shut with night
we lie together but something
keeps us apart.
                    Turn off the heater,
lose your form in its
receding glow. Shadows move out
from corners to cover everything.
They snatch you from me
like insects like men pawing
for your dark body.

We

We pare an apple
We drink a cup of
orange juice
We sit on a bench
We go to a coffee bar
listen to the lark
the spring lark
We play with
each other's

hair
We plodge in eddies
of Love

there is a particular
and definite
glory

about the simple
things we do . . .

Artful, The Blonde Instant

Constriction of blood,
our articulate vessel
pieces together failure of the
body,
  to keep up with the flow,
  the cinnamon tune of may.

She carries on the simple
constriction of my heedless
manner,
re-directs the vessel
down the soft channel
 which is her hands or hair,
& she does careless things,
artfully,
walks across the street,
footprints dressed in red.

Drums

a blood orange sliced
 in three on the dresser
  lace curtains rhapsodic
   with wind our lips

   respond like
   Romany
   tambourines

A Valentine; For Ever

Quick the hand that deceives the thigh
      as thrush, birdlime,
mellowed from ages in loam,
tulips on the skin, drives to perfection
struggling black hair.

A vague mouth lifts to the sky,
breathes deeply, evening deep.
the Heart acquaints with the power
of the deceptive fuse.
Quick the teeth to catch the cheek
(Poet in a lime of love
sings whistles dances oh so
joyously)

Now no time to set the rhyme
working, placed on the glacial
stair moves several years a day.

Dawn—purity feloned from
a time replaced.

Position to lip, grasp quill, scroll, take chart
to the sea, sail off

Read the verse of the wind in your tresses!
Accept no break from this storm
Even when the whale returns home
Mullet wash your eyes with bleary
scales.

Knuckles of thought raining
into the sheet-hard limb

Quick the hand that deceives the thigh
Cunning the heart that shrugs your love

Instead of a Ring

With hardness of tin
   your eyes cut
      my body's length—
         tongue burns in your
            beautiful place
               (tender figure throbs with
                 labour of lovemaking)

             ashes to ashes
              teeth to glass

                Electricity!
                Burning satin!
                prowling in
                your thighs

              Harness me to
             this milky yoke
           work me
        grind my bones

       to seed you, softbelly,
     thin hands,
   and your blonde tresses
  bleeding onto the pillow,
Vivienne

The Boy From The Green Cabaret
Tells Of His Mother

June to July 1967

each steel line fur to the wrist,
each man his own judgement,
to re-spirit the heart, churn the
vein roughly
to the platform of the muscles

it is a case of musicality and historical chance.
Kent in hazy june,
over the points,
        urgency in each nerve

look south look south
to the web about St Paul's
its scaffold crown
        hatching a blue sky
its engineers spidering the street

time is spared the honour
of rushing after.

    London air is clear, not sharp,
Compton St strippers
lack urgency they deserve,
cooly ask for sandwiches and beer

Rimbaud and Verlaine
swaggered in these same alleys
& the sun for Verlaine's rosary
after a lover's row

each friend away
from my outstretched hand,
and from my reason   oh
        tell me it is not so

Sealine

woman lies on a couch of misery
with her dreams.
oh fertile architecture that replenished my eye
in dockland, where knotted groups
of pickets shook me as a friend
& grabbed my shoulders bruising me even in
their union strength. oh those cold lands i
must cover before she will rest in peace
on the shingle that clacks on the hulls
of Cuban sugar ships,

the weak brine of the thames as oily
it oodles round the wharfs. those delicate pebbles
and shells and waves those masts and store rooms
those cruel times by
the sea's foundation

Bladder Wrack Blues

the sea is pregnant with bladder wrack
your bed was a groaning ship sounding
out the ocean floor

your house was a box where i kept my shoes
your chairs were bright blue & electric
but that was yesterday that was tomorrow
& never today

A Letter, This Far Away, Tonight For Liberty

I

walking to post the other letter
its form exact in my pocket & the sun
behind chimneys
& round the corner it splashes on the
trunk of a single oak,
                    trickles through fences
                    dappled in tiny ivy diamonds.

2

a pine cone
rolls towards me
turns upside down
and stands in my palm with the
chunky stance of a screech owl

slits under its mail
give it the effect & carriage
of a Samurai—
    a pine cone rolling
    at the feet of every man,
    sodden with many trampled streets,
    never inquired after.
so Benno Ohnesorg, I dream of the spirit
and fracture of the one-month-old sacrament.

I stand alone in the Krummen Strasse,
whirlpools and windmills ahead of my feet.

the apex of the spirit and flesh dont stand
a chance in the arms of Moloch.

a cone rolls across Europe from this tree
where I stand beneath the sun, sets over
west Berlin,

a white mark on the curb,
a red mark on the spare ground,
the oak tree a fabulous truncheon
the black acorns are thunderclouds over Europe

One Year Old, The Wilted Hybrid

in this town bushes are a second warmth.
   in this town everyday there is no
friendship
         & a blanket
   of events curtails us:
   seeing the galaxy as a red
truth cast on poor soil
  on a poor root of person
     who all belong somewhere else yes
   they all belong elsewhere.

the flower-delicate mind is a
     replete dormitory
shaped against actual climax
     or climatic sweat, a gin distillery
is the heaviest industrial concern,
     and that phrase photographs the replete
        heads,
           companionship we lack

a dream so far in me as to be in my
very arteries. quilts of rain lashing into
        peat, a light-handed wind picking
    drops off juniper clumps.
    ruinous action and other friends
    inside these houses   ,
                        as if hydrogen
        were the entire possibility
    into spaces, this town sleeps day in
        night outside is broken
    by loudspeakers, speak-easy is the
tongue of this town, the alfalfa, chlorophyl
        shining under the canopies
    in the precincts.

ii
    cobbles tramlines & winkle packets
        budgie eggs in sawdust, shredded tobacco
in a faltering hand, an unerring man. steamy
        nosed children of this city,
        dazzling dark. it could be 1926 another fantasy.
        the children of this town are
                not of this town, principally.

On The Burning Down of the Salvation Army
Mens Palace, Dogs Bank, Newcastle

They stood smoking damp and salvaged
cigarettes mourning their lost bundles,
each man tagged OF NO FIXED ABODE.

Mattresses dried in the early sunshine
blankets hung over railings and gravestones
water and ashes floated across the cobbled hill.

A tinker who wouldn't give his name
bemoaned his spanner, scissors and knife-grinder,
which lay under 30 tons of debris.

Water on the steps in the dining room
but none to make a cup of tea

Tangled pallet frames smoked still,
men lounged around mostly in ill-fitting
borrowed clothes other naked in only
              a blanket or soaked mac.

We looked at the scorched wood and remarked
how much it resembled a burnt body later we
heard it was charred corpse
we remarked how much it resembled burnt-out timber

The Axe

as an instrument
& means of persuasion
lacks elegance:

its affections are
over-lustful, its
attentions are soon ended,
its face too polished,
too chic & its look
is criminal

but the tongue
with its silver
bushels of dainty
                    lightning,
cracks the woodblock
of evil down the centre,

showing the grain.
here we find the poet
stamping out fires made
by the wood-shavings from
other mens heads.

The Boy From The Green Cabaret
Tells Of His Mother

Lady powders the nourishing teat
in her platform of bricks.

Vapour, azure smoke, ash
drifts over the gravel-pit.
A blond boy gossips with carp & tench.
His mother, draped black, traipses mountains
for her sergeant-at-arms.

A grizzly kiss is Liberty.
A drunken hug is worth a revolution.
Trumpets blast! Bugles wallop out a reveille!
—it is an urchin wiping her nose on rags—

My sleeping-bag is the Plough, slicing
cloud-pillows, nightcaps from moonrays!

Rain, cheap beer—
White thunder on my collar—
A boot next to my heart—
kicking over bowers & stadiums—
Fabulous underground rivers of foxgloves—

The mail-coach upturned,
wheels spin like planets,
poems pinned to its shafts!
Dames, merchant, musketeer,
in the dead season.

They lodge in a liver-coloured
slab-drab morgue, eyes shooting out
red as radishes! Flesh tinted
with the gradual shellac of Death.

The Poet scrawls his testament—
his ink freezes, jelly mixture of soot
and red wine. His ranks are deplete,
the chains of his body jingle.

Grapeshot tatters canvas, cold is
bone-deep; the black widow flounders,
the river sucks out her unbroken maidenhead;
she screams wildly—Delight!
The blond boy knots his handkerchief,
tears up newspapers, picks louse off his neck.

He turns over sees a glass of electric violets.

The Copper Heart

prisoners & brides tear at geraniums
its copper wings in the bars of their heads

marine chariots of pearl and tungsten
poems drizzling from fat volumes

tulips drip blood gouts
children pick sunshine adults burn bread

lets tear down forests drink the sea
dry take off every stitch of clothing sprawl   in the corn
    madness

poems for Miss Selaneus, courtesy of Madame John

The Temper

Do not touch me with casual
vagaries—clouds, deltas, the
organic machine of the cockroach as *super-*
humanly it prods an ashtray across kitchen
tiles—oh no, I won't strike
the anvil without white heat, nor
watch the scarlet cloud, symbol
of my every free desire, turn black,
and symbolise the captivity of my every
evil caprice. I examine the life-pushers
at work, industrious as the dung-pushing scarab,
but with a capacity for idiocy unequalled
by the entire insect world, as
sea crashes into white flakes of land,
dissolving over millions of light lives, each Christmas
  star no
  more than the tinsel we trail
  through love, or our affectionate
  quality. We
  dissolve if we are not alight with
  the blaze of change—as the sign is
  a bodily health of communing
  thousands, and
not the stringent occasion of return. A star shines
over this place that went out two light
years ago, too many million lives ago, as we survive
  in the path of
  history.

Exotic

I sailed on blue oil, and of the
Coconut. Tygers and monkeys
Stared from Rousseau's jungle,
And I landed.

There grew harebells of brass
Where I trod.

I saw you dance the ritual,
Your thongs flung the sand!
Your wet thigh, garlanded symmetry—
Your white yucca skirt!

Oh Yadwigha! Yadwigha!

Your heart
My lust
so we are alive.

The Holy Net

Through the grid, the aluminium glint
of the dead, and blood-washed animals.

Naked men shout they are poets and
prophets, but they are no different from you,
or me. Animals limp back, master-less; salt
wears at the bullocks lather. The grid
opens its teeth to a world of unfamiliar
people and kisses. Jesu, Jesu, speaking
in the one language I understand; of
hymns, for peace.
Across wasteland, crystals
ice over the heads of dead men.

In this beautiful terror, I speak
a gentle language with her.
Silence.

A Lovely Child

she spat through her teeth,
delicately, as the novel would
invariably say

this one pulled up her
white
        dress
peed against the sea wall
   jaunted into the port
whistling a hymn
through her teeth

2nd Telephone Song

Emeralds, spa-rock chips
quartz slivers if all these
fell on this same stretch
of black straight path &
rickety hedge none cd
compare with the
cracked gaunt slip of finger
nail pointing as
some bright star thru
years and years & joy
along which we sailed
in eyes of storms in
sunshine & rain
(yr bright fingernail
brings yr voice past
terraced wardrobes a
grocery store the motor
way to this humble bright
& oh so willing nest
of outward going concern
for you for you for you

The Margin

a violet springs for sunshine, through
a brown crust, making a shadow & making
      colour in a mans eye, like a mans promise
  or his poems. the air is creased with
    january's cold—part of the stream ices
over. we take off our heavy overcoats, hold white
        mugs to warm our hands, and drink mush-
          room soup, dipping yesterdays bread in it.
we dry our hair with a blue towel, and there is no special
        magic between us that makes me pick
    a withered dogrose from the rosehip cluster & put it
behind your ear. a man is more than that—he is
        the sum of his wants, & more acutely
    pure, is the sum of his needs.
    i dont need you, you dont need me, and we steady
our wants in that: real as the quartz on the
        sill, real as the snow on the porch,
      as the fire that is burning out
    because there is no coal.

The Decision, Finally (for Jeremy Prynne)
4 am, March 24 Sparty Lea

And we have the decision,
which was ready made,
    and now its clear
    and, as they say, cleared up.
What have we to fight for,
save books, and contours,
and the tidal bore,
and the way we behave?

we have the decision
without bitterness, with
a *resignation*
to the facts which are *these:*

      there is a land, a people,
      among ourselves, too, for
      this a legacy, already
      said,
         the golden legacy,
      to beat into coin.

I am a minter of coins.
Let's not forget that.

The Pain of Beauty

The delicate torture is *accepting*
pain as pleasure,
               silencing each
other with words that reflect our lightest
stroke or touch. There is no alternative
to death. Clouds touch the corn
fields of Northumberland. Clouds smash into the
dark torment of a mans body, as
we squash our own rebellious fires,
kicking the dust of history over them.
The general failure
       is that we never make it possible
for ourselves
to alienate the plight of a stray tomcat from the
lot of any unemployed south american miner,
with a tall hat, greasy sideburns &
LESS money than it takes to starve.

ii
A woman has a dark face at night
but her touch is light. Like a gunshot
or an *epitaph*, (a black contusion on the
back of a stone, a tall heavy stone),
or a
     Hymn of the Republic that
Guevara sang, as his blood sang,
as bruises swelled and the mouth distended with
red heat,
as those arid plots of land, contorted
       beyond all human effort or possibility
lie beneath the Bolivian sun.
Like dead potatoes, like a swift fish or
an
    execution, or a kick in the ribs,
to crack whatever silence, to glorify
whatever
        & however hopeless a cause for freedom.

Song

The visitor sat with me
Days and nights—gold as a finch,
Black as a gun barrel, inquisitive
As a child.

After a fortnight of insomnia, it left the
Vermouth, the glasses, the
steam, and a grey longing.

Is this freedom?
This grey longing?

Sometimes, it returns, when it is
Raining, and there are lights in the street.
And in men.

And I ask it to believe me when I shout
That you are beautiful and that I
Worship you.

Chansonette at 1.20 a.m.

most things these days are big
Mahalia Jackson, Robert Morley, John James,
Paul McCartney's head, dole queues, pay cheques
everything is big or fat there is no finesse in
such fleshiness there is no substitute for
lack of curvature or petite people & things
such as goldfish or valentine-cards
Who wants to be big I don't who wants to
be as tall as a Haarlem Globe Trotter or
as fat as Orson Welles I dont
Twiggy stay as you are it's the only way we'll survive

When Paul Woke Up Today & Put On His Clean White T/Shirt

snow was crisp on the lawn at
dawn as I got up & popped the cork
in the remaining VERMOUTH bottle
draining off the dregs to get rid of
the taste of spring onions & black
pepper. at 6.30 Paul turned over & sd
     Hey how do you do it smelling
of drink this early? He thinks me
foolish yes I am a fool Yes
I do love him

After Breakfast (With Peter) Costing 5/6d.

a girl in a hooped miniskirt leans against the white door
of the CLOTH MARKET CAFE
its 10.30 a.m. here are cabbages jewish
artichokes granny pippins & button mushrooms

its so sunny. i spat blood
but i'm smiling now
in my soul i have yr photograph
you lying on the bed with coy curls
its in the fly paper of VOGUE magazine

walking past the GREEN MARKET i saw you no
it was a vision an
out of date Christmas tree
because

you too were tinsel & bonnie lights & streamers & presents

& Evergreen

Death Go Get Yr Shoes Repaired & Mend Yr Icey Hat

Sergei spoke poems to Isadora across
    a sunbeam copse & Nijinsky
was not going to bed with Diaghilev.
        tonight the sky is washed with blue
  significant or not of a dark past—
the coolest stars are blue.
       She stumbles down the dark
steps in the derelict part of town glowing
    with cider its so good to drink flat & stale
beer for her to smoke too much. She hangs on to
      the scaffolding—Gods of the steeps help
  us! There are no cats in this part of town &
No i dont think its dangerous to
         burn quickly but try telling
    Joan of Arc that, she had a trueblue
  belief in fire brigades.
  oh Woman of the ice (yr heels click,
my future is in my raincoat pocket, its yr hand.
    & after both deciding not to jump into
  the Tyne, content with spitting in it, we
walked off in the february frost—

i kissed you for the first time in the
middle of the Swing Bridge in between two counties in
order to spread the loveliness over as
much ground as possible
. the usual drunk & old
woman on the last bus West bangs her synthetic sealskin
boots against the seat sides & sings songs of the 1920s
What is it that makes me sing silently in my
furry lungs You ask me to hold yr hand
i really mustnt but you tempt me with instant
coffee & the sweet peasant Tibetan smell
of hot milk & coffee
(you sip coffee & i still have the taste of China
tea in my mouth What tastes! We shall start
a cafe solely for lovers lips)   & later walking
home alone & taking an hour over it to savour
it all
i skipped down the bank towards the
roundabout & thought:
it *was* all the same places, the same bars,
the same beer, the regular bridges and familiar
streets and churches and the same people.
But believe me when I say it was different.

Love Poem (for you)

I am no tsar
in a winter palace

I have no balalaika
to play a melody
in the tents
of Serbia

my sole virtue is
in my hand

Invisible as a swan
        on ice
noble as Corinth
fishermen

Love, in my hand I have
the answer
    the response to a silver
    prayer

I have no lute
to string you
a melody of silk

I have a poem
before my eyes
    a song in
      my mouth
My love for you
is not elaborate

It is unleavened and
    enough

break it
    and eat

Touching

we are young dont touch us
we make love & we are refreshed
sing to the colours of february, fast
for a fortnight against the latest
war knowing we cant change you
(i am told it is hip to do
                              this) we
are strong & we ripple dont touch us
we prefer watching the darkening
of the elderberry than staring at
the latest drama on CORONATION ST.
or the newest crisis on THE NEWCOMERS we
love sunshine even when
we are blind DONT TOUCH US for
you will certainly break & we dont
want your brittle death on our hands
as even now on our hands we have
yr brittle life

To Me Mam, Somewhere To The North Of This Shit

I

Even dark North Sea fish are
caught in the net of the absentee landlord
whose province is not land but total
possession of the soul
        (butterflies & princesses
lie deflowered in the snow) I mutter a cold prayer

2

Women stem their blood flow for love &
cry about their children at night in
the lonely lovers bed
which I taste & you taste & we all taste
which is beyond the holiness of their
position & possessions   me mam is a
stooping figure shovelling coal from
the path into the cellar & she
worries, not like a hound worrying a rat, but
       like a star worries
    the ocean,
who fears no reflection